WEARING A
COLOSTOMY BAG

BY HARRIET BRUNDLE

KidHaven
PUBLISHING

HUMAN BODY HELPERS

Published in 2021 by
KidHaven Publishing, an Imprint of Greenhaven Publishing, LLC
353 3rd Avenue
Suite 255
New York, NY 10010

© 2021 Booklife Publishing
This edition is published by arrangement with Booklife Publishing

Edited by: John Wood
Designed by: Danielle Rippengill

Find us on 🅵 📷

Cataloging-in-Publication Data

Names: Brundle, Harriet.
Title: Wearing a colostomy bag / Harriet Brundle.
Description: New York : KidHaven Publishing, 2021. | Series: Human body helpers | Includes glossary and index.
Identifiers: ISBN 9781534535565 (pbk.) | ISBN 9781534535589 (library bound) | ISBN 9781534535572 (6 pack) | ISBN 9781534535596 (ebook)
Subjects: LCSH: Colostomy--Juvenile literature. | Medical instruments and apparatus--Juvenile literature.
Classification: LCC RD543.C6 B78 2021 | DDC 617.5'547--dc23

Printed in the United States of America

CPSIA compliance information: Batch #BS20K: For further information contact Greenhaven Publishing LLC, New York, New York at 1-844-317-7404.

Please visit our website, www.greenhavenpublishing.com. For a free color catalog of all our high-quality books, call toll free 1-844-317-7404 or fax 1-844-317-7405.

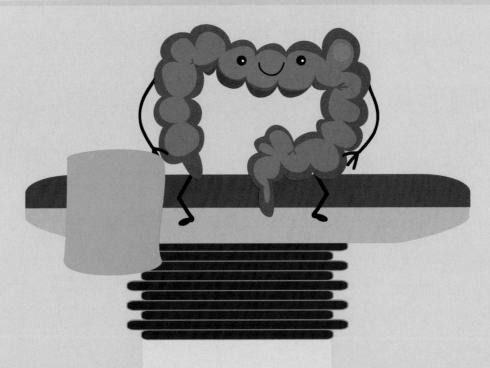

IMAGE CREDITS

All images are courtesy of Shutterstock.com, unless otherwise specified. With thanks to Getty Images, Thinkstock Photo, and iStockphoto.
Front Cover & 1 – Beatriz Gascon J, NikaMooni, rumruay. Carlos – Beatriz Gascon J. Charlie – rumruay. 2 – Zentangle. 5 – Beatriz Gascon J.
6 – Zentangle. 7 – Beatriz Gascon J. 11 – EstherQueen999. 15 – Zentangle. 18 – EstherQueen999. 19 – WindAwake. 22 – flatvector.

CONTENTS

Words that look like **this** can be found in the glossary on page 24.

WHAT IS THE COLON?

Your intestines are a long tube that connects your __stomach__ to your __anus__.

Your intestines have two parts: the small intestine and the large intestine. The main part of your large intestine is your colon.

Hi! I'm Carlos, and I'm your colon.

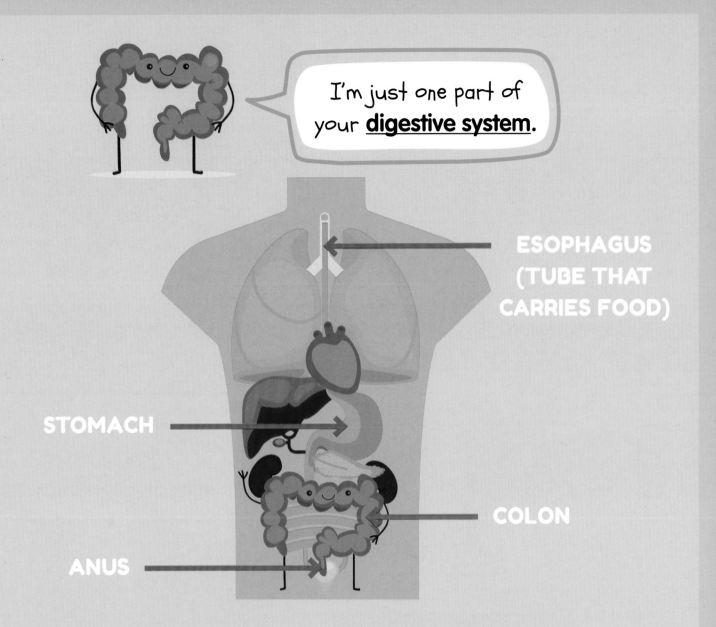

Inside your colon, any waste that your body doesn't need is formed into poop, also called stool. When you go to the bathroom, your body is getting rid of the waste.

WHAT IS A COLOSTOMY?

A colostomy is an **operation** in which a part of your colon is cut and pulled through an opening made in your skin. The operation is done at the hospital.

Don't worry! You won't feel anything during the operation.

The opening is called a stoma. After the operation, the waste you would usually pass from your anus now comes out of your stoma.

Your stoma will usually be pink or red in color, like me!

WHAT IS A COLOSTOMY BAG?

Hi, I'm Charlie, and I'm a colostomy bag.

A colostomy bag is a small bag that attaches to your stoma. The bag is used to safely collect the waste that now comes from your stoma.

Colostomy bags are waterproof so they don't leak. Many bags also have a filter, which means that other people don't notice any smell. The bag is small enough to wear under your clothes.

9

WHY MIGHT I NEED A COLOSTOMY BAG?

There are lots of different reasons why you might need a colostomy bag. You might have a problem with your colon or have an injury or illness that means you can't pass waste normally.

Ouch! This is painful!

If you feel pain or have problems when you're going to the bathroom, it's important that you tell an adult. It might not be a problem at all, but it is always best to be checked by a doctor.

WHAT HAPPENS AT THE HOSPITAL?

Hi, Carlos. I'm going to be your colostomy bag. My name is Charlie.

Hi, Charlie. It's nice to meet you!

The doctor might say you need a colostomy operation at the hospital. Before you have the operation, you'll be told all about what's going to happen.

After your operation, you may need to stay in the hospital for a few days. You'll be given medicine, usually through a **drip**, to make sure you're not in any pain.

It won't be long before we get to go home, Carlos.

While you're at the hospital, you will be shown how to take care of your stoma. It's really important that you keep the opening clean so that the skin doesn't become **infected**.

A special nurse will show you how to empty and change your colostomy bag. If you have any questions, the nurse will be able to help.

WHAT HAPPENS AFTER MY OPERATION?

After you have had your operation, you might find that your colostomy bag takes a little bit of getting used to. You might feel some pain at first or feel very aware of your bag.

You'll soon get used to me, Carlos!

The doctors will tell you the foods you should and shouldn't be eating.

FOOD

YOU CAN EAT

DOCTOR

You may need to change what kinds of foods you eat after your operation while you get used to having a colostomy bag. You should be able to eat normally again after a few weeks.

HOW DO I CHANGE MY COLOSTOMY BAG?

When you need to change your colostomy bag, make sure you have everything you need ready before you start. Wash your hands, and carefully peel off the used colostomy bag.

It's really important that your hands are clean before you start.

Clean your stoma gently with warm water or a wipe, but try not to rub the area. Once the skin around your stoma is dry, you can carefully stick on your new colostomy bag.

DOS AND DON'TS

DO make sure when you leave the house that you, or an adult with you, have everything needed to change your colostomy bag.

DON'T get any creases in the part of the bag that sticks to your body.

DO remember to clean your stoma every time you change your colostomy bag.

DON'T forget you need to change your colostomy bag as soon as it starts getting full.

LIFE AFTER YOUR COLOSTOMY BAG

In some cases, a colostomy operation can be <u>reversed</u>. This means that your colon is **<u>reattached</u>** and you can poop as you did before you had a colostomy bag.

Some people will need to have a colostomy bag for the rest of their lives. For most people, once they're used to their colostomy bag, it doesn't affect day-to-day life too much.

GLOSSARY

ANUS — the opening in the bottom where waste leaves the body

DIGESTIVE SYSTEM — the parts of the body that work together to break down food and produce energy

DRIP — a small tube put under the skin to deliver medicine right into the body

INFECTED — affected by a disease

OPERATION — something done on a body to remove or mend something

REATTACHED — being attached to something again

REVERSED — put back to how it was before

STOMACH — a sack-like part of the body through which food passes

INDEX